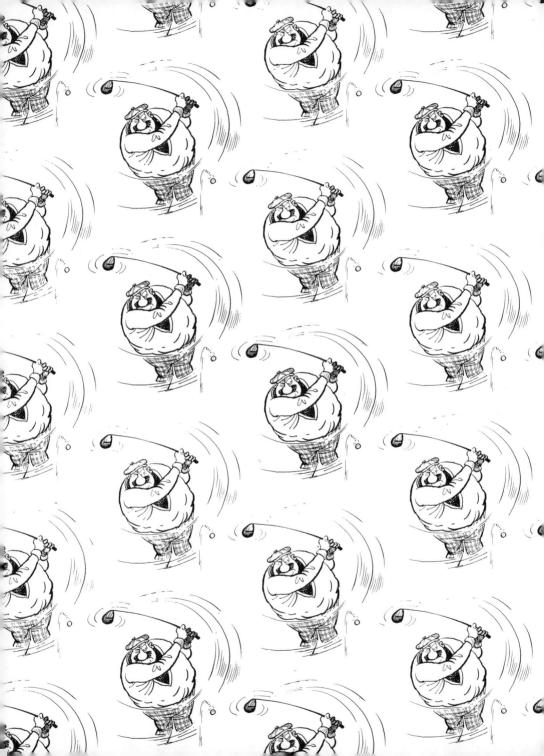

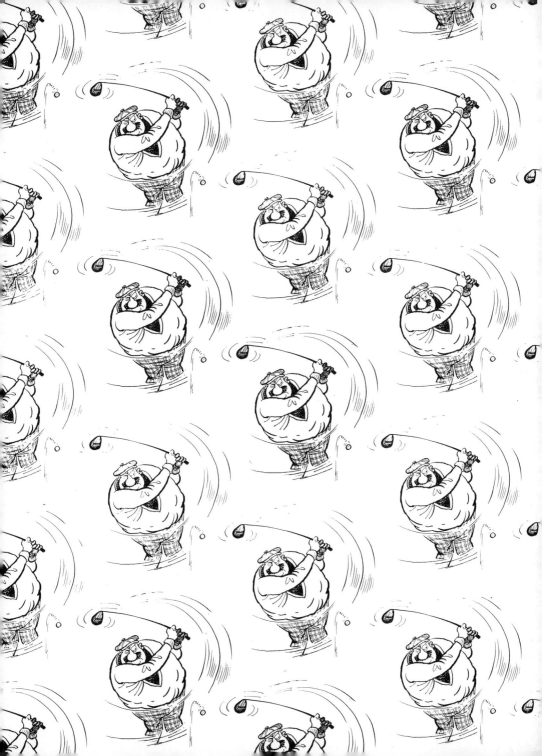

YET MORE BEDSIDE GOLF

Peter Alliss was born into golf. The height of his
playing career came in 1958, when he won the Italian,
Spanish and Portuguese Opens in three successive
weeks. Today, he is the doyen of golf commentators
and as such is regarded as the rightful heir to Henry
Longhurst. His television programmes *Around with
Alliss* and *Pro-Celebrity Golf* are the most popular of
their kind. His other books include *Bedside Golf,
More Bedside Golf, Play Golf with Alliss* and
An Autobiography, all available in Fontana.

Peter Alliss
YET MORE
BEDSIDE
GOLF

Illustrations by S. McMurtry

Fontana Collins

First published by William Collins 1985
First issued in Fontana Paperbacks 1986

Copyright © in text Peter Alliss 1985

Made by Lennard Books,
Windmill Cottage, Mackerye End,
Harpenden, Herts AL5 5DR

Editor Michael Leitch
Designed by David Pocknell's Company Ltd
Production Reynolds Clark Associates Ltd
Printed and bound in Great Britain by
William Collins Sons & Co. Ltd, Glasgow

CONTENTS

Preface

elcome to yet another thought-provoking bundle of observations about our great game, the people who play it and the people who watch it. In this book our main theme is how the game has changed – how it was in the 1890s, in the Twenties, Thirties and Fifties, and how it is now, seen in terms of clubhouses, caddies, club secretaries, spectators, the average club golfer and his eternal needs. We also wonder if some of the fun isn't going out of golf. Perhaps more people would benefit from sharing the attitude of the airline pilot who wrote these words to me:

'Time and work determine that – enthusiasm undampened – I play, at most, three rounds a year, and from any one of these I seek only one good drive, one good iron, one good putt, and one good hole.'

Sir, the game needs more like you.

All in a Good Cause

ake two magazine covers. The first is Vol 1, No 1, of *Golf*, published on Friday, September 19th, 1890; the second is the December 1983 edition of *Golf World*. Compare the plain type of the first with the pin-up pose of Jan Stephenson in the second, and it is clear that ninety-three years is a long time in golf!

But has the game changed all that much? Are things really all that different for the average club player for whom such magazines were invented? This is a theme I want to look at from several angles in the course of this book, for there can be no single hard-and-fast answer. What interests me most is the idea that a lot of things in golf are very much as they used to be back in the days of the hickory shaft and the earthen closet which doubled as a dressing-room.

Changes there have been, certainly, but if you prod about for a while in the various highways and byways of the game you often find that these changes are small ones – no great revolutions, just practical ways of keeping up to date with the world outside.

Television has had an enormous impact, of course, making the game much 'bigger' than it ever was. But this impact, if you analyze it, has been very largely at tournament level. I am not at all sure that television has greatly affected club players in the way they approach their own game – give or take a few bad habits, which we shall return to later!

Let's look for a moment at golf equipment. The pages of a magazine such as *Golf World* are a regular Aladdin's Cave of bags and boots, clubs, balls and umbrellas, practice nets and putting machines, exotic holiday offers, and beautifully photographed reminders to lay in a case or two of that other great Scottish export. All very enjoyable – especially when winter has taken its grip and daydreaming in a favourite armchair with a glass of the amber fluid seems almost better than tramping those soggy fairways down the road. Nevertheless, seductive advertisements in the golfing press are hardly a new idea.

Back on Friday, September 19th, 1890, the editors of *Golf* were already dab hands at the armchair-shopping game, even if the technology was a little more primitive. Prominent among the ads in that very first issue was one for the Eclipse Golf Ball – complete with standard Victorian warning to 'Beware of Imitations' – and another for the Wimbledon Club Carrier, a waterproof marvel to be obtained from 'all Indiarubber Depots' (where are *they* now?). There were no glossy enticements from the liquor trade, admittedly, but other splendid comforts were on display, e.g. Thompson's French Corn Plaster ('Since using this Plaster, I can walk almost any distance' – Lady Maude) and Kola ('The Golfer's Friend'), a nut-based substance which a homeopathic chemist with branches in Glasgow and Edinburgh was urging on all who took 'prolonged physical or mental exertion', especially golfers and cyclists.

So that side of things has not changed much. There's just more of it about today. Let's look at another area. Let's take, if she'll pardon the expression, Jan Stephenson herself. Here I will allow that your average male golfer has not long been exposed to delights such as that magazine cover (and the calendar, by all accounts, went like hot cakes in Japan). One of the main reasons for this change of direction is that, for many years, women were not encouraged to believe in themselves as golfers. There have always been outstanding individual players – Lady Heathcoat-Amory (Joyce Wethered), Babe Zaharias, Catherine Lacoste and many others – but they were exceptions in a man's world, and were treated as such.

Only when the present generation came to the fore, with women such as Jan Stephenson and Nancy Lopez, was it possible for tournament organizers, sponsors and the press to think in terms of big money for women golfers. By then, thanks to television, tournament golf was established as a big-time commercial product, with a galaxy of spin-offs which now happily include colour snaps of Miss Stephenson holing out in a wind tunnel.

'Miss Higgins'

Commercial pressures make Jan Stephenson's life a frantic year-round chase from one venue to the next. Back in the old days, the strictures were of a different kind. As the Fashionable Lady at the City Golf School cried:

'What? Grip the stick with both hands? And how, pray, am I to hold up my skirt?'

A knotty problem indeed, and one which the splendid Mabel E. Stringer remembers in fine detail in her *Golfing Reminiscences:*

'How on earth any one of us (in the 'nineties) ever managed to hit a ball, or get along at all, in the outrageous garments with which fashion decreed we were to cover ourselves, is one of the great unsolved mysteries of that or any age … I can remember when the sleeves were so voluminous that we always had to have an elastic strap round the left arm, or we should never have seen the ball at all.

' "Miss Higgins" (named after the American golfer) was indispensable on account of the width of the skirts. This was an elastic band which was slipped round the knees when the player was addressing her ball, and was the most useful as well as the most unsightly of the many inventions to counteract the vagaries and inconsistencies of *la mode…*

'The golfing girl of today should indeed be grateful that she need not play golf in a sailor hat, a high stiff collar, a voluminous skirt and petticoats, a motor-veil, or a wide skirt with leather binding.'

Mr Harbottle's Instruments

I don't think we can quarrel with Miss Stringer's verdict. And yet, going back to my earlier point about changes in the game, the more I delve into the historical aspects the more it strikes me that the *spirit* of golf – the fellowship, the

competitiveness, even the humour – has barely altered in the last hundred and fifty years.

In 1968, when The Old Manchester Golf Club reached its 150th birthday, a celebration dinner was held at the Grand Hotel in Manchester. For the menu card, someone had the bright idea of reproducing extracts from the club's early Minute Books, and some of the findings appear below. The language may be a little archaic, but I hope you will agree that the essential feeling behind the words is no different from what you would hope to find at your own club.

'Meeting. 4th December, 1826:

Mr Harbottle with the Irons only v Mr Connell.

The best of eleven holes, one shilling the hole, one crown the match.

This match excited considerable interest from the singularity of the instruments used, and many bets were made. The first hole was won by Mr Connell, the second by his antagonist and so continued in favour of Mr Harbottle who gained a match of four at the tenth hole.'

'Meeting. 18th December, 1929:
The characteristics of this meeting were Frost and Snow, neither of which deterred the Gentlemen from showing themselves hearty in the cause – the Snow being upwards of four inches deep.'

Now comes our first meeting with the mercurial Mr Gibb. We know nothing about him as a man, but it is always fascinating to speculate beyond these little snippets.

'Meeting. 13th August, 1830:
Burt and Andrew v Gibb and Fraser.
Best of eleven holes, 1/- the hole, half sovereign the match.
This match was won easily by Messrs Burt and Andrew. Mr Burt in capital play, Mr Gibb quite the contrary.'

Now we move on a year, and there seems to have been little improvement in poor old Gibb's game.

'Meeting. 16th September, 1831:
Burt and McHaffie v Fraser and Gibb.
This match was badly played by Messrs Fraser and Gibb, their opponents winning a bumper.'

Dear, oh dear. I wonder what Fraser thought about it all. Should he ditch Gibb and find someone more reliable? Perhaps they were both getting on a bit, and stuck with each other. Here's a clue:

'Meeting. 20th July, 1832:
Allan v Gibb.
Best of eleven holes, 1/- the hole, half sovereign the match. Mr Allan to be allowed four strokes in the round.
This match was well contested and at the eleventh hole both parties were even. Mr Gibb, however, not liking the idea of being beaten by a younger member, came in the winner by one hole.'

Good for him! His game may have been fading, but still there was life in the old dog. He'd show those young whippersnappers! What is more, as the next entry shows, he was still bucking the odds five years later.

'Meeting. 8th June, 1837:
Hunt v Gibb.
  Best of eleven holes, 1/- the hole, half sovereign the match.
  The odds were 5 to 4 against Mr Gibb at starting but Mr Gibb, not liking to be so little thought of, did his best and gained a match of four.'

He must have enjoyed that one. The club secretary, too, or whoever wrote up these notes, shows a quiet sense of humour which I find very typical of a certain species of clubman, and very English. But perhaps, on reflection, he was *not* the secretary, for in the old days the golf club secretary was a breed apart, and not renowned for his good humour.

Achtung! Visitors!

The old-time secretary was a demi-god. Retired from the services, usually the Army, with a rank somewhere between captain and brigadier (major-generals and above were a shade too lofty to wish to supplement their pensions in this way), they were walking flamethrowers who cut swathes of fear in the ranks of ordinary members as they prowled the corridors of the club – *their* club. As for visitors – *what?* Humiliation was too good for such people. As for foreigners – *whaaaat?*

I am thinking of one particular fireball at this moment, but his line of attack was typical. You could have written to him from the United States five years before, stating your wish to play at his fine club on Thursday 14th May and that you would like to start at 10.30. You would receive a brief note of acceptance, and every year you would send a reminder, which would be acknowledged. At last, on the great day, you arrive and announce yourself to the secretary.

'Good morning, Sir. I am James Burnett from Knoxville, Tennessee...'
'Never heard of you!'
'Well, I've received a whole bunch of letters from you...' You wave the sheaf of letters.
'Don't know anything about them!'
'But...'
Protests are in vain. Your only hope is to wait, while the *monumental*

inconvenience which you have caused is digested. Then, after much blowing through the nostrils and pacing about, he may say:

'Oh, all right! I'll have a look.'

Files and ledgers are brought out, opened and pored through. At last, if he has found you, he will sullenly mutter: 'Hmmm.' But this is only the overture to his triumphant next move when, wheeling on you, he barks:

'You're late. Look.' He jabs at his wristwatch. 'You've missed your starting-time.'

You are in no position to argue that any delay has been his fault, not yours. You are actually grateful when he says:

'Get here late, I don't know. You'll have to start at the 10th. Only nine holes. I'll see you about this when you come in!'

He turns and strides towards his office. As he approaches the door, he passes a member of the club who cheerily calls to him:

'Good morning, Colonel. Nice day.'

Through gritted teeth the secretary snarls: 'I haven't had time to look out of the window.'

As you head for the locker-room, you at least have the consolation of knowing that you are not alone.

Another secretary of the old guard will never be forgotten because of the gigantic pair of binoculars which he used for scanning the course. Real U-boat commander stuff. If you went into his office to arrange a game, he would walk to his window and sweep the fairways with these enormous binoculars. From his vantage point he – and you – could very well see that there were no more than four or five players out there.

'Hmmm,' he would say at last, lowering the glasses and shaking his head. 'We're very busy this morning. Very busy. *And* I've got someone else coming at half-past eleven.'

'Well,' you say respectfully, 'I do see the problem. But it is still only ten o'clock.'

'Hmmm.' The great man ponders. Then, abruptly: 'Come back in fifteen minutes.'

It was just like school in a way. The daily tyranny of a prefect over his fags. Nowadays it is very different. The larger golf clubs are turning over big sums of money, perhaps half to three-quarters of a million a year, and the secretary has to be more of a businessman, gathering and chasing up subscriptions, looking after the takings from green fees, the bar and the one-arm bandits, plus the expenditure on the golf course. All this amounts to a demanding job which really should be done by a man with proper business qualifications.

There is also the question of staff. These larger clubs need more people to help run them, and today's staff would not be content to be ruled with the kind of military one-sidedness that was standard behaviour with the captains and colonels. Times have changed. All the same, I miss watching the old boys at work. They were, in their monstrous way, very good value. But I fear we have seen the last of them.

Then There Was the One About...

One day in 1909 a pretty girl was having a golf lesson. She looked deeply dejected.

'It's no use, McPherson,' she cried, 'I'm afraid I shall never make a golfer.'

'Naw, miss,' replied the pro, 'ye hae the hecht, an' ye hae the swing, but ye've nae the heid, ye ken.'

Did you get it? No? Well, it's hardly surprising, since it's almost another language. 'Heid', you see, is 'head', so the old pro is saying that the girl may be all right in some departments, but she doesn't have the brains to be a golfer.

That kind of joke was the staple of golfing humour for many a year. Rude Scotsmen had the field to themselves. Whether they were caddies, pros, fierce red-bearded giants, icy advocates or some other species of black-coated worker, they used a terrible venom to paralyze their victims, who were either ignorant twits from across the border, or women.

As the game spread beyond Scotland, the old jokes were modified so that the newly converted could understand them. Example:

A visitor to Westward Ho! asked his caddie the name of the water which had to be crossed at the last hole.

'Some calls it by one name and some another,' said the caddie. 'It depends on the circumstances. There's an old Scottish gentleman, and when he gets over it he says he has "carried the burn". But when he tops into it he says: "Pick my ball out of that damned sewer!"'

The Scottish flavour was still there, but now more people could understand the joke. As time went by, Scotsmen were actually removed completely from some jokes. In one 1930s variant on our 1909 joke, an Eastern potentate was receiving golf lessons from a cockney caddie. The caddie was teaching his pupil to drive.

'That's right, yer majesty, keep yer eye on the ball. Slowly back, yer honour. Pause at the top, yer highness. Gordon Bennett! Yer've missed it again, yer silly black bugger!'

So we go on. New jokes do get invented from time to time – think of all those Celebs and their scriptwriters slaving away to outdo each other on Gala night. By and large, though, I don't think that the basic humour of golf has changed much in the last century. Presentation, the way jokes and stories are told – that has certainly speeded up, but in essence it's still the same old sitcom with a new twist, or a variation on some familiar disaster which has just happened to one of the members at the club, or to his wife, dog, etc.

I can only think of one type of golf humour that could be called new. It comes from the United States and it reflects their world of anxiety and analysts, where obsessiveness and 'inner golf' are keywords to understanding even the ordinary club player's attitude to the game. For example:

Doctor: 'It might improve your health if you took up golf.'

Patient: 'But I do play golf, doctor.'

Doctor: 'In that case, you should quit.'

Some of their fantasies are a little bit wilder than ours:

First golf widow: 'Tell me, Mary, how do you get your husband to come to bed?'

Second golf widow: 'That's easy. I have a nightgown made of astroturf.'

And some American stories are just a little bit on the black side:

'John, you promised to be home at five and now its nine-fifteen.'

'Honey, I know, but just hear me out, will you. It was Charlie ... Charlie is ... he dropped dead on the 8th green.'

'Oh! But that's terrible!'

'It certainly was. For the rest of the day it was: hit the ball ... drag Charlie ... hit the ball ... drag Charlie ...'

Now, I'll wager they don't tell stories like that up at Royal Dornoch!

The Sound and the Fury

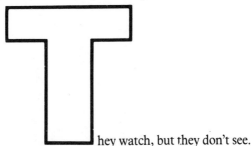

hey watch, but they don't see. They listen, but they don't hear. It is quite extraordinary how many letters I get from people who clearly have been looking at golf on television, but can never get the details right. Or even the basics.

I and my fellow workers at the BBC are frequently praised, and condemned, for work that we haven't done. It was on ITV.

They say: 'Why don't you do something about Ben Wright?' Or: Why do you have to have that man with the white bit in his hair (Dickie Davies) introducing the golf?'

Or they get something else wrong. They say: 'I have watched all your Pro-Celebrity matches at Gleneagles this year.' They weren't; they were at Turnberry.

They say: 'I watched your *Men versus Women* series with great interest. I thought So-and-so was excellent, but Whatsisname didn't have a clue.' All the names are wrong. Some of the people may have been on a previous series; others – so far as I am aware – may never have picked up a golf club in their lives.

They say: 'Mark McCormack was on *all day* from the Open Championship. Why do we need an American voice...?' You check back, and you find that over the four days of the tournament Mark was at his seat for four hours, so he may have spoken for forty minutes altogether.

Do you get my drift? Short on accuracy. Perhaps I am being a shade hard, because many of us are prone to making sweeping statements. But I do sometimes wonder what is going through people's minds when they make these funny connections. In a sense they are like one of my more regular correspondents. He too is a golf watcher, but the game is really a kind of dream machine for setting him off on his favourite track, which is religion. Within the space of three or four lines, he can move from considering Greg Norman's tee-shots to the inner meaning of Romans, Chapter 8. It doesn't bother me – whatever turns you on, kind Sir – but it's not exactly what the programme planners had in mind.

With all this going on, it is good to know that there are some true golf enthusiasts out there, who get very fiery when their favourite sport has to share the afternoon or evening with other events. In particular I am thinking of the viewer who wrote to express his disgust at the BBC's presentation of golf. On the Saturday the Open had apparently been interrupted no less than eight times and, he claimed, the eventual winner was barely seen at all. On the Sunday the golf had been taken off to show *motor racing*. There were, he supposed, people who *liked* motor racing.

Stars and Garters

Of late, motor racing has had more stick than other rival attractions, such as cricket or tennis. With some viewers, the true issue is not the sport itself but the narrower one of how much exposure their own private hero is receiving. Of the serious golfers, Greg Norman is now very well supported, and Sam Torrance is beginning to climb the fan ratings (I wonder what that pencil behind his ear is doing to help the cause).

Of the Celebs, Sean Connery arouses the most excitement by far. Or seems to. If you disregard the fanatical outpourings of a certain family from Streatham Hill, the picture might well be different. I wonder that some of their missives get through at all. The whole family has a go, and they write on both sides of the postcard. The main message is usually on the back, but they can

never get it all into the space, so they overflow on to the front, run round the address, and finish by patching any remaining white space with slogans, such as: 'NEVER MIND THE WOMEN – JUST YOU CONCENTRATE ON OUR IDOL' and 'WE HAVE OUR EYES (AND VIDEO) ON *YOU*'. Not the sort of thing I would choose to read at breakfast, but as a commentator I have come to accept that some people think you also edit and direct the programmes, as well as being Head of Sport, Head of Television, and Director-General of the BBC.

Nor is it wise to make personal remarks about the stars. Someone's idol always turns out to be someone else's demon:

'Dear Mr Alliss,

How dare you compare the lovely face of our Nick Faldo with that awful thin-lipped beady-eyed Jimmy Connors. I suggest you have your eyes tested.'

And that was from a '62 year old grandmother golfer (h/cap 19)'!

No, the only personal remarks that no-one else minds are the ones aimed at the poor old commentator. A few years ago I was berated for appearing on the screen wearing a coat and no tie. 'I wonder what Longhurst would have said,' wrote my critic.

A low blow, and I was sufficiently provoked to send him an answer. On the whole I feel that ties are the neatest solution (Henry would have said the *only* solution; he was not the type to entertain either a polo neck or a sports shirt). I forget quite why I was so casually turned out that day, but I remembered a more embarrassing moment from my youth, and offered that by way of an explanation.

It was down at Wimborne in Dorset. An old friend had died, Ken McIntyre, professional at the Broadstone Golf Club, and a clash of dates meant that I had to play a round of golf before I could go to his funeral. I was delayed on the course, and by the time the round was over there was nothing for it but to dash straight to the funeral without changing. In the churchyard I stayed well in the background, but as people left the graveside and began talking in groups I kept apologizing to anyone I met for my appearance. This went on until one of my old mentors from Ferndown put an arm round my shoulder and said:

'I am sure the Good Lord and Ken are pleased that you've turned up to pay your respects. What you wear is neither here nor there. It's what's in your heart that counts.'

I smuggled some of this into my letter – and was forgiven by return.

A Dog Called Wogan?

It must have been the Year of the Dog somewhere. Viewers have suddenly been noticing that dogs not only appear on golf courses, they do so during televised matches. Some dogs even appear by invitation!

'Dear Mr Alliss,

I thought it was quite wrong that you, and the Gleneagles Golf Club, should allow James Hunt to bring his dog on to the course. Surely we have enough trouble in public places with mess created by dogs without our having to suffer it on Golf Courses too.

Yours etc.

PS I hope that neither Hunt nor Wogan will be invited to take part in any future televised games. They were not pleasant to watch.'

Strange. I always thought James's dog was called Oscar! My favourite letter on this subject came from J. Dixon of Chorley, Lancs:

'Dear Mr Alliss,

As a golfer and an avid viewer of all golfing programmes I would like to draw your attention to a situation which is creeping into the game and, in my opinion, could lead to unfortunate incidents, or distress, to the professionals whose livelihood depends on the game.

'I refer to the growing practice, by the public, of taking dogs on to the course, also the practice of cameramen and your good self of drawing attention

to these pets. The present series *Men versus Women* is an example, when twice you drew attention to the dogs and at one point passed the remark, "There is the obligatory dog!"

'Golf enthusiasts are recognized as a considerate, well behaved crowd, and are fully aware that even the click of a camera at the crucial moment can distract the player and cost him a stroke. What then if a dog suddenly barks? Bearing in mind that one home in four owns a dog, can you imagine the situation if at the Open golf tournament, where there are 10,000 spectators, a quarter of them decided to take their pets – that would be 2,500 dogs! If one person is allowed this liberty it is surely to be expected by the rest.'

Over the top? Well, maybe; but you have to remember that the whole business of dogs on golf courses is fraught with double-dealing and hypocrisy, and always has been. Consider the secretary's dog.

Of all the non-human animals you will find at a golf club, the secretary's dog is the most sacred. It doesn't matter that dogs have long been barred from the course, the secretary may have three. *And* they may be large and unruly, *and* charge about all over the place, pinching golf balls and worse.

One of the famous tyrants I mentioned in the last chapter – we'll call him Colonel Driver – had a black labrador. A visitor arrived at the club one morning and went to call on the secretary to see about a game. With him he had a new Burberry raincoat and a new Burberry bag. He set these down on the ground just outside the door of the clubhouse and went inside. The secretary's office was a couple of yards down the corridor leading to the men's locker-room.

The interview went well. The chap had played at the club several times before and knew Colonel Driver. What's more, Colonel Driver even admitted to remembering him. So, feeling quite pleased with the way it had gone, and looking forward to his round of golf, the chap stepped out of the office and went to collect his kit.

He opened the clubhouse door and found the secretary's labrador piddling over his new Burberrys. As he approached, the dog turned his head and gave the chap a rather disapproving look, and kept his leg up for a few more seconds.

I was in the clubhouse at the time, and when I heard what had happened I sympathized with the Burberry-owner. 'Hmm,' I said, trying not to laugh, 'that was a bit strong, wasn't it?'

'Well,' said the chap earnestly, 'I think I was lucky not to get a bollocking from Driver for leaving my kit in the way.'

You could hardly ask for a finer example of the true power of the old-time secretary!

Watching our Language

It may seem churlish to say so, but in my experience there is no more treacherous device a correspondent can use than to open his or her letter with a bouquet of warm and flattering sentences. 'Thank you for another splendid series … We do admire your deep knowledge of the game, we appreciate the sympathy you bring to explaining its finer points, and your Confucian understanding of the player's point of view…'

The old commentator's eyes narrow as he reads on, waiting for the moment when the dagger will be drawn and neatly slipped between his ribs. Ah, here it comes. The old commentator sucks in his breath, ready to absorb the blow.

'…One small black mark. Your expressed hope that Craig Stadler might "get his ball in the hole" – from his bunker-shot at the 18th on the final day.

'IN is a preposition indicating a PRESENT relation to (space).

'INTO is a preposition expressing MOTION to a point within (space).

'I love Americans but I hate Americanese…'

Pronunciation is another touchy area, especially with viewers who had the good fortune to study some foreign tongue – Spanish, German, etc. – and have remembered what they learnt. Thus a Mr Goddard from Harrow insists that we at the BBC start describing a certain young German as 'Bairnheart Lung (as in lung)-er'. He goes on:

'The BBC's German Service will confirm it. After all, they (the Germans) wouldn't dream of calling you "Pater Ulliss".'

I am not so sure about that. I have been called one or two strange things in Germany. In any case, the average British viewer is not very hot on languages, and if we start rolling our r's, and hawking and lisping all over the place to try and imitate the way they pronounce a player's name in Dortmund or Santander, our average viewer's reaction is likely to be 'Who the bloody hell is that?' – because the name we have just spoken into the microphone bears little relation to anything he can see on Harry Carpenter's scoreboard or in his daily newspaper. I think, in fact, that we do better by not going overboard with foreign words. There is a kind of mid-Channel compromise for some of the better-known ones, and that is perhaps as far as we need to go. Any further, and you get statements like: 'Welcome to Mathreedth, where Se-ve Byos-terros is fighting to preserve a two-shot lead over Hosay-Mareea Cannythareth and Neeg Phalldo – sorry, Nick Faldo.' I hardly think that would be of lasting interest!

We are, however, always open to informed advice. I was both glad and touched to receive the following from a Mrs Hope in Gullane:

'Dear Mr Alliss,
On behalf of the people of this village will you please let it be known in your TV commentary that Muirfield Golf Course is at Gullane, East Lothian.

'It is most annoying to hear it repeatedly announced that the Open is being played at Muirfield as though that is the name of the village also.

'I have today heard of a young foreign lady who requested an Edinburgh taxi driver to take her to Muirfield without any mention of the village. Unfortunately for her she was left at a bus stop in Portobello and told to find her own way from there. Luckily a young lady found her crying and managed to put her on the right road.'

Lucky, too, that Scottish hospitality came up trumps in the end.

Please Borrow my Husband!

The search never ceases for new Celebs and new faces to appear on the more light-hearted golf programmes. Unfortunately, there are what a BBC Spokesman might call 'overriding factors'.

The power-that-be, the accountants and the dreaded ratings list demand that on our 'fun' programmes we must have good runners alongside me who can both play reasonable golf and be articulate. The BBC has considered all kinds of suggestions about inviting club players – male and female – up to Gleneagles. But there are problems. Even the showbiz people get nervous about appearing, but they at least are used to handling crowds and big occasions. Someone who is not used to it might be terrified out of his wits. His game would seize up and he would hate it all.

The other problem comes when I say: 'Well, George, and where did you learn your golf?' They go white and reply: 'Guurrghhh...' followed by silence. Not ideal for television. Nevertheless, the search goes on, and we have had some very interesting guests on *Around with Alliss*, even though the bias is perhaps towards people who are public figures.

I am delighted, all the same, to receive letters from sponsors of every kind, especially if they are as lucid as Mrs Joan Watts of Maidstone:
'Dear Mr Alliss,
I am a golf widow, but I can stand that. What I can't stand is being an unwilling participant in Pro-Celebrity Golf. It's not so much the golf and it's certainly not your lively commentary, it's the constant heckling coming from the chair next to me that drives me to drink.

'My husband can't understand how your celebrities can have such low handicaps (meaning lower than his 11) and play so badly (in his opinion).

Whichever poor celebrity takes the field, be he American or British, he is always branded "no good".

'I have tried to explain that nerves, playing with the world's best and the presence of a gallery and the TV cameras must have an effect. However, my "know it all" states that playing with a better player should improve one's golf.

'Please – if ever you are short of a celebrity, use my husband. Just so that he can have a taste of the pressure and strain, so that he can fluff his drives and miss his putts and perhaps then I could learn to enjoy golf – IN PEACE!!

'Yours sincerely, believe me!'

Madam, I do believe you. Sincerely. But have you tried Noel Edmonds, or *Game for a Laugh?*

Who Can You Turn To?

o sport can ever have had as many prophets as the game of golf, each with a different message. They can't all be right – can they? One of the problems facing the club golfer in his local library, or reading his Sunday newspaper, is that not all advice is good for everyone. He must somehow select what he feels makes sense for his game. Provided it is not too much at odds with what his local pro has been telling him for years, he should be all right. (Not that the local pro is *always* right – but he *usually* is; that is why he is still in work.)

Sometimes it is possible to weed out certain prophets on the basis of old age. When they wrote their books they were playing in a different era, with different equipment, and their laws no longer apply. The old-fashioned clubs were long and had hickory shafts almost as thick as cricket bat handles, and the only way to hit the ball with any power was to sweep at it with a scything motion. If you chopped down on it, or were too upright, the ball would just pop up in the air and roll a few feet.

Hickory shafts were difficult to live with in other ways. There was good hickory and bad hickory, and if you had managed to collect a few good clubs, it certainly paid to look after them. The clubhead might get twisted and then everything would go to pot; or a shaft might suddenly break. You may have thought a certain shot was on, that you could force the ball out of that rut, then half a minute later you are holding a fractured club in your hands, and remembering the wise words of Dorothy Campbell-Hurd:

'In order to learn a sound method of hitting the ball it is absolutely essential to have clubs that balance well with each other and have a similar line.'

Exactly. And now you have bust that favourite iron, where are you going to find another piece of hickory to match up with all the others? Life could be tough in those days, when matched sets were but a far-off dream.

So how would today's player cope with the old conditions? We tried a little experiment some time ago at St Andrews. Jack Nicklaus and Ben Crenshaw played a few holes with hickory clubs. Nicklaus could not master

them at all, and ended up taking eleven or twelve shots on one hole – which made him pretty furious – whereas Crenshaw with his broad swing got the hang of it very quickly. Of course, Crenshaw was putting his great knowledge of the history of the game to work, but it was still impressive to see a man turn back the clock with such apparent ease.

The lesson is obviously to be wary of books dating much before the 1920s and '30s if you are looking for tips on how to play. Compare this piece of advice from James Barnes, who was at his peak in the early Twenties, with current thinking:

'When the hands get in front of the swing as the ball is being struck, you can look for a big slice nineteen times out of twenty.'

Now that may have been fine using the equipment of his day, when you had to keep the hands behind and throw the clubhead at the ball. But if you look at modern pictures of Palmer, Nicklaus and Watson, their hands are well ahead of the clubhead at the moment of impact, and of course that is because they have all the benefits of steel shafts and modern technology.

Barnes was playing at the end of the hickory period. Steel shafts were creeping in and were legalized in 1929. Soon the talk was not of sweeping but of hitting down on the ball, which had not been possible before.

Charles Herndon wrote: 'If the professional can be said to have secrets of success, then by far the most important one of them all is their habit of hitting down on the ball.' P.A. Vale agreed: 'Scientifically speaking, the most perfect golf drive should be hit downwards and perhaps to a lesser degree all golf strokes unless on the green.'

In the old days they were much more obsessed with getting power into the drive. James Barnes again: 'Start the club down slowly, then speed the clubhead up gradually to where it is travelling at the maximum speed just as it reaches the ball.'

The great Harry Vardon was much of the same mind: 'Go slowly back but be quick on the ball, yet do not swing back too slowly or lose control over your club. Gain speed gradually.'

Wanda Morgan, a famous British and English Ladies' champion of the Thirties, recognized that the times were a-changing, but was all for giving the ball the best possible whack: 'Contrary to many expressed opinions, I think hard hitting is an absolutely necessary factor.' Of course, she was wise enough to emphasize the importance of *good* hitting, not just wild bashing: 'Length without direction is a snare and a delusion,' she wrote.

The Pit and the Pendulum

When it came to bunker play, the old-timers were of one accord: your only chance was to thrash your way out of trouble. As James Barnes put it:

'Swing round upright for an explosive shot out of the bunker. Keep your head still and tear into the sand at the back of the ball. Don't try to follow through.'

Not much subtlety there. But then the bunkers themselves were not as sophisticated as they are today, and the sand-blaster had not been invented. So

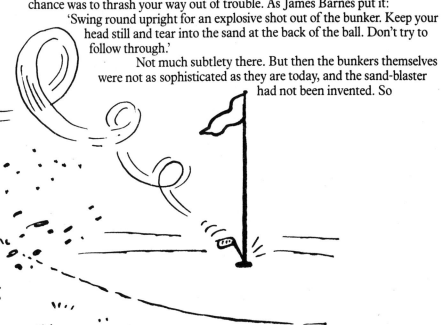

the old technique was to smash and tear into the sand, in the hope that the sand would pile up on the clubface with enough force to throw the ball out.

The next changes in the theories of driving arose from a blend of nature and science. They turned on the notion that if you brought the club down in a more natural, unforced way, this induced a pendulum effect and the clubface would be travelling with maximum force at the point of impact.

Once it was established that you no longer needed to belt the cover off the ball, the debate turned to finer matters of rhythm, coordination and timing. S.F. Kern had a good motto – a bit deep, but very sound:

'So here is the secret (for me) of golf. Mentally, follow the progress of the clubhead during every moment of the swing.'

On the other hand, is it for you? According to Alex Gerard: 'The mental side of golf has the majority bunkered before they even start.'

It's even worse with putting, but we deal with those very separate arts in a later chapter. Meanwhile, I am with Florence L. Harvey when she wrote: 'Science against brute force applies to golf as well as boxing.'

The trouble is that Golfing Man (*Homo Paganicus*) is an ambitious animal. Tommy Armour, that fine Scots-American teacher and player, well understood this when he wrote:

'One of the greatest menaces to good driving for the average golfer is that he is never satisfied with the length he gets from a well-hit ball.'

By and large, when playing into the wind, the pundits have all seemed to agree that you can overdo the force. Chick Evans, the great American golfer who in 1962 played in his fiftieth consecutive US Amateur Championship, said:

'If you are playing in windy conditions, don't try to hit too hard into the wind. Then, more than any time, the rhythm should be perfect and, when it is, wind will not affect the shot.'

I am not convinced that following Chick's advice will tame the wind on every occasion, but he has a very good point. A shrewd man of today, John Jacobs, offered a more challenging solution:

'When you are trying to play into the wind, don't hit it harder, try to hit it better.'

Relax and Enjoy It

Grantland Rice, the eminent American golf writer, was a firm believer in all-round sanity and control, and his advice is good for any day of the week:

'Put the main control where it belongs, into the hands, wrists and arms. Keep the body as relaxed as possible and give the idea a chance.'

Now that, I know, is very much Henry Cotton's thinking. 'Whatever kind of grip is employed,' wrote Henry, 'always hang on at the top. This will at least cut out one source of error.' Remember, too, the words of Walter Hagen:

'The timing of the stroke is done as much with the feet as with the hands or the body.'

Ernest Jones had a slightly more negative way of emphasizing the value of footwork: 'Anything and everything may happen to the golfer who tries to root himself to the earth. Anything and everything but good golf.'

He had another theory: 'Control in the fingers and freedom everywhere else, that is the doctrine.'

Not quite the same as the Grantland Rice theory, but not so very distant from it. Freedom and relaxation are the keynotes, and these also form the essence of what Bobby Jones believed. On the subject of hitting power, he said:

'No-one ever swings too slowly. Over-effort is the cause of the average golfer's trouble.'

Or, put another way, the average golfer lacks patience. He can't wait to see his ball flying down the middle of the fairway, so he cuts corners to make the dream come true – and pays for it. As H.B. Martin put it:

'Waiting for the clubhead to come through is one of the most difficult things we have to do in golf.'

I will buy that. I will also buy something else that Bobby Jones said – even though it may seem to contradict his earlier statement about over-effort:

'An excess of caution is not a good thing,' said Jones. 'It leads to steering and quitting on strokes.'

I don't think the two are basically at odds if you take the combined meaning to be: take your time, but go for your shots. He is really trying to find a way of getting people to play sensibly; if they do, then their confidence will naturally increase. Jones also made an important distinction between light-hearted and serious golf; the latter had an extraordinary physical effect on him, far removed from anything the Sunday golfer might or should expect to happen after his weekly round.

In 1919, Jones lost eighteen pounds during the six days at Oakmont. In 1925 at Worcester in the Open Championship and play-off, he lost twelve pounds in three days. He also spoke of the 'furious toll exacted from the spirit'.

To Sway or Not to Sway

Competitive golf at the level of a Jones, Hagen or Nicklaus is not our main concern here. What we are looking at is the way the principles of play have

changed over the years, and we seem to have come through all that barrage of advice to two main conclusions. Firstly, players have always had to modify their game whenever there was a fundamental change in the equipment available. Secondly, many of the old maxims about concentration, relaxation and confidence hold good today, fifty or sixty years after they were first written.

If only it was all so easy. If only golf was like a board game, and there was just one path through the trees to the treasure chest on the other side. But, as all you dedicated followers of fashion will be aware, golf – and life – are not like that. What is right for George may be doom and disaster for Harry. And long may it be so. Golf – and life – would be infinitely tedious if all things were equal to all men.

I was reminded of one of golf's more shadowy areas by a viewer's letter which took me up on remarks I had made about Tom Weiskopf's swing. I had referred to its beauty and effectiveness, but also wondered if there was not a touch of sway in it. 'When I started to play golf forty-five years ago,' the viewer went on, 'I was strongly urged to avoid sway in my swing. People like James Braid and Abe Mitchell were cited as exceptions to the rule.'

The answer, of course, is that there will always be exceptions. There are too many ways of playing golf well. The great swayers, or lateral movers, in my time were the amateur Joe Carr, Fred Daly, and Peter Thomson who had a very marked sideways movement. There is even a hint of it today in Tom Watson's style.

Ben Hogan had a different idea, and this too may have been all right for some but not all. He thought it best to put the weight on the left side as quickly as possible, and leave it there. This was in contrast to the other school which swayed back and then moved into the ball. Hogan felt he was better off being forward already and over the ball, rather than having to move away from it to play the shot.

In fact, the difference between the two styles, spread over the driving actions of a dozen golfers, is pretty fractional. The main point is that people have always looked for a chap with a *new* idea. New is good. It may solve their problems, make them better players...

All this theorizing drives some people potty, of course, and this too has its funny side. It was Jock Hutchinson, British Open Champion in 1921, who growled: 'More practice and less theorizing would help a great many players.'

Well, bless his heart, I think what really happens is that people do their theorizing and then go out and try to practise it. There's no point in whacking balls around without a good idea of what you are trying to achieve.

Finally, to come back to the title of our chapter –'Who Can You Turn To?'

– it is surely one of the great ironies of golf that so many of the famous players who have written books – Ben Hogan, Bobby Locke, Lee Trevino and Jack Nicklaus will do for starters – were themselves unorthodox in some way or other. And yet, when you read their books, they describe the way to play as if they did everything in a perfectly orthodox manner. Bobby Locke in his book never mentions that he used to draw the ball in about twenty yards from right to left; what he describes is how to drive the ball dead straight. Nicklaus says nothing about why his right elbow sticks out the way it does; Trevino does not think to explain why he aims so far to the left. They must think they are normal!

So there you have it – from the mouths of Champions. 'Do as I say, not as I do.' Is that clear?

It Shouldn't Happen to a Caddie

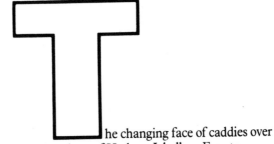

The changing face of caddies over the last thirty years has been nothing short of Hyde to Jekyll, or Frog to Handsome Prince. Back in the Fifties most caddies – apart from those reared in the ways of the old school, at St Andrews and the other great Scottish courses – were layabouts and villains, dropouts and tramps who slept under hedgerows and drank cider or meths by the quart. I doubt if there are any left today. They have been replaced, thank God!

The new caddie is clean, presentable, aged about twenty-five and all fired up with enthusiasm for the game. There are a number of Irish boys, Americans, Australians, even New Zealanders, plus a few English, Welsh and Scottish lads, and through their caddying they are able to travel the world – unheard-of thirty years ago. A caddie with a passport? He would not have known how to get an application form, let alone fill it in.

The change did not come about overnight. It was a creeping process which began when it dawned on some of the older caddies that they were worth a bob or two more to the people who employed them. They weren't just porters, they actually *knew* the courses, and this knowledge was valuable – not only to the touring professionals but also to ordinary club players, whether they were local members or visitors. People were taking their leisure more seriously, and becoming more competitive. Thanks to the influence of television, they too wanted to be Arnold Palmer, and if they couldn't quite hit the ball as well as Arnie, at least they could get themselves a caddie who knew how far it was to the hole and could advise them about their shots.

Over the next few years, some of the sharper caddies began to fancy themselves as technical advisers – men who could expect to earn a decent wage from golf, especially if they could bring home a few winners. The trouble was, they had no standing in the game, either with the clubs or with the tournament organizers. The powers-that-be regarded them as little more than beasts of burden, and never thought to offer them any facilities on the course. Golf was still run on feudal lines, and the boss class was highly resistant to change – rather like the old mill owners who might have saved themselves a lot of trouble later if they had paid their workers a little more at the time.

The Tent

The first concession that I can remember was at Moor Park. Someone, at last, had responded to the caddies' requests for somewhere to put their gear, and have a drink and a sandwich. The result, however, was like the opening offer in a six-month series of wage talks. It was a tent. It was about twelve feet square, with a sign outside which said: 'Caddies'. Inside was a bare trestle table – and that was it. There was no-one to look after any gear that might be left there, and not even a jug of water on the table.

The caddies' response was predictable and unanimous. 'I'm not bloody going in there,' they said.

A strange kind of guerrilla warfare broke out, as the caddies started hanging round the back of the clubhouses, scrounging mugs of tea and whatever else was going – except that they didn't want to pay the same price as the members, they wanted canteen rates.

This did not automatically win them a toehold in the clubhouse, but a process of infiltration was launched. Social conditions were changing, too. Rates of pay improved, and then the tournament timetables were reworked so that, on the final two days, play was limited to eighteen holes instead of thirty-six. This gave the caddies time to make their own arrangements, to go back to their digs and have a meal instead of being stuck all day on the course, where the price of a ham sandwich was no laughing matter.

The popularity of golf went on growing and growing. Now the caddies were appearing regularly on television, and all this fame and exposure encouraged them to become smarter and better-educated; soon the students were moving in. You have only to watch the Open Championship for a few minutes to see what I mean.

This new breed of caddie is keen, smart, agreeable, does his homework – and is sometimes allowed into the clubhouse! Many people thought that was the thin end of a rather nasty wedge, but it has turned out quite well. After all, if the

WONDERFUL IN THE CLUBHOUSE,
....COMPLETELY HOUSE-TRAINED.

caddie is as bright and well-dressed as anyone on the course, why shouldn't a player be allowed to bring him along to the bar and the restaurant. I cannot think of a good reason – and yet I must say I have some sympathy for those who oppose such changes. It may be reactionary, but there are a lot of club players up and down the country who prefer their golf – and their world – the way it used to be. Some of them would claim – and it is hard to disagree – that the game was more fun in the old days.

In Scotland they still order things on more traditional lines – and perhaps this is what guarantees Scottish courses a regular flow of enthusiastic visitors every year, many of them from the other side of the world. It is certainly true that most of the old caddie stories emanate from Scotland.

In the Days When...

The young caddies at the golf club were firmly controlled by a strict but benevolent caddie-master, and the greatest event in the calendar was the caddies' annual treat. One year the caddie-master said to a small boy with a large appetite:

'Will ye tak' anither bannock, Archie?'

'Naw,' said the boy.

'Naw?' repeated the caddie-master, offended by the boy's abruptness. 'Naw – what?'

'Naw, dammit?' cried the boy. 'Are ye deaf?'

Whisky Galore

Even the youngest caddies were no angels. They were training for a tough trade – out in all weathers, the size of their tips depending on the quite accidental matter of whether their man could play golf or was a hopeless idiot. In most of the hallowed Scottish caddie stories, the punter is definitely in the second category, while the caddie himself is a neglected philosopher who has seen everything.

A visitor to Troon was driving very erratically, and on every hole was in the rough on one side or the other. He complained to his caddie:

'Caddie, the fairways on this course are exceptionally narrow.'

'Aye,' said the caddie, 'very narrow, Sir. A lot of people think it would be better to bring the rough to the middle and shift the fairways to both sides.'

A nice whimsical touch there. More urgent was the plight of the old caddie at St Andrews. He was carrying double for two Americans. It was a foul, dreadful day, cold when they set out, then at the fourth hole the rain began and the wind got up. Raindrops were soon coming down like machine-gun bullets, and one of the Americans pulled a bottle of whisky out of his bag, took a slurp, handed the bottle to his friend, who also took a slurp, then the bottle was returned to the bag.

The Americans repeated this ritual with the bottle about every two or three holes. The rain lashed down, and they had reached the sixteenth hole when one American turned to the old caddie and said:

'Jesus, isn't there a dry place on this goddam course?'

The old caddy looked at him, the rain dripping off his nose, and replied: 'Aye, well, there is just one. Why don't you try the back of my throat?'

The uses of 'usquebaugh' in golf were, and are, many and various. As the caddie at Carnoustie explained to his client, when cleaning iron clubs there was nothing quite like a drop of whisky.

'But how do you use it?' asked the client.

'Well, Sir, I drink the whisky and then breathe on the heads of the clubs.'

Of course, the experienced caddie always knows how to put overbearing or difficult clients in their place. A posh novice had just picked his ball out of the hole at Gleneagles on a wet and rather muddy day, and was looking down at it with some distaste. His caddy sidled over and said to him, in a confidential tone:

'I wouldn't lick my balls if I were you, Sir. They've been putting wormkiller on the first four greens.'

'Oh. Er. Yes. Er. Righto, Caddie. Quite.' The words accompanied by a look of sudden horror and confusion.

Every golfer must start somewhere. But perhaps it is a good idea to postpone the Scottish golf holiday until the rudiments of the game have been learned. At all events, never be apologetic in the hearing of a caddie. Never, for instance, say:

'I suppose you've seen worse golfers in your time ... Ahem, Caddie, I said I suppose you've seen worse golfers in your time.'

'I heard you the first time, Sir. I'm just trying to remember.'

No novice, in fact, should ever involve a caddie in unnnecesary conversation. I always think of the visitor to Musselburgh who confided:

'Actually, Caddie, I took up the game as a way of learning self-control.'

'Ye should have gone into caddying, Sir,' came the reply.

I also think of the slow player who was having a dreadful day at Troon. His shots were going all over the place, but what annoyed him still more was the attitude of his caddie, who followed him everywhere in total silence, and from time to time stole an ill-concealed look at his wristwatch. At last the player could hold back his irritation no longer.

'Caddie,' he cried. 'I do wish you would not keep looking at your watch.'

'It's not a watch, Sir,' answered the caddie. 'It's a compass.'

Musical Interlude

olf has produced only one song of its very own, so it is a special pleasure to set this lilting rarity before your eyes. My thanks to the Reverend Peter Gedge of Hutton Buscell, near Scarborough, for sending in the words of:

'TAK' TENT YE BLITHE BILLIES'
A LAY OF THE LINKS

Tak tent ye blithe billies wha drive at the ba',
And dinna think strength is the hale o't a va'.
A Samson like felly may smash through the green,
The airt o'ts the pairt o't whaur gowffin is seen;
Yet its no in the arm...the e'e or the leg,
If they work na as ane...ye're no worth a feg.
Like clock-work a' bits o' the body maun gang,
Then strike her ma hearties she'll mak' the recht sang.

CHORUS:
Gin ye want to be young...and no to be auld,
That yer bluid may run warm...instead o' deid cauld.
Tae be canty and crouse...not dowie and dowf,
Take an auld man's advice...and learn...tae gowf.

II
The king o' the body has aye been the heid,
If the ruler is bad, but sma' is the speed:
Gin ye want to be far, and aye to be sure,
Forget nae, my lads, to think a' in your pow'r.
A pompous professor, ance breaking his club,
Received frae his caddie this pertinent snub –

"For Latin and Greek, Sir, ye may hae a heid,
But for playing at gowff it's brains that ye need."
Chorus –

III

Your young anes think driving will win them the game,
The auld pawky putter can bring them to shame;
Some swear by the iron and on the cleek lean,
Play weel wi' them a' ere ye challenge the green.
In making your matches tak' care what ye do,
Weel made they're half won, is a saying that's true,
Mind this abune a', as the very best rule, –
Ye're no worth a preen if ye dinna keep cool.
Chorus –

IV

Gan cannily on, let this not be forgot,
Because then ye have time to study each shot:
The man in a hurry can never dae weel, –
He'll heel her, or tap her, than a's to the deil.
Wi' clavers and havers ne'er spoil a guid game,
Much crackin' while playing will never bring fame; –
When dune tak' a drap frae the auld tappit hen,
And then is the time to fecht battles again.
Chorus –

Pros and Cons

n the early 1950s Henry Longhurst wrote a small pamphlet called 'Unwritten Contract'. His purpose was to remind the members of golf clubs that, without their continued help and support, the professional could not afford to exist. As Henry put it:

'...The professional, while a "servant of the club", is not paid as such. He is paid a retainer. With very few exceptions you may take it, never perhaps having inquired, that your professional is retained at between £2 and £5 a week.

'If your club is a biggish one, he will have to keep an assistant. The assistant will be paid, almost certainly, £5 a week – *by the professional*. From the professional's point of view this simply does not add up. How then is he expected to live?

'The answer is, from the proceeds of an unwritten contract which has existed between members and their professional since the earliest days of golf. It is this unwritten contract to which I here respectfully draw attention.'

Henry went on to build a miniature portrait of the professional's working week – seventy hours long, sunrise to sunset, no lunch hour, fifty-two weeks a year, club shop stocked out of his own pocket, performs innumerable small services for nothing, sometimes doubles as part-time greenkeeper and caddie-master as well. And so on. That, then, is the pro's contribution. What about the members? In Henry's own words:

'The member, on his part, undertakes to patronize the professional and his shop to a sufficient extent to provide him with a living. That is all.'

This means, in essence, buying your kit from him and not for a quid off in the sports shop down the road. That is the nature of patronage. There is nothing quaint or medieval about it – it is just an honourable way of balancing the books. It is also sensible for newcomers to take lessons from the pro, so if you have a son or young friend coming along, guide him towards the professional. Henry Longhurst recalls that he had his first golf lesson on the fifth day of his golfing life. He was smitten, and spent the rest of his school holidays either having a lesson or waiting impatiently for the next one.

The other reminder he makes in 'Unwritten Contract' is to play with the pro. His fee is 'about equal to that of an indifferent London caddie. Shared among three in a fourball it is negligible – but what a lot he will give you in return.'

Indeed, and the principle is very much with us today. The pro at your club will probably not make regular appearances on the tournament circuit – that is one of the major changes since the Fifties – and needs regular practice to keep his own game in trim. Meanwhile, for a few pounds you and your partners can give him a game and very likely learn enough to knock off a couple of strokes overnight. It's the kind of deal that should leave everyone feeling that they have done well out of it.

Balancing the Books

I have been a close observer of golf club economics all my life. In my father's day, at Ferndown where we all moved in 1939, the pro could make a comfortable living. Eighty per cent of the pro's earnings came from the active members, that is to say, from about 150 of the total of about 400 members. Other earnings might come from summer visitors to the Bournemouth area, and in winter a few still came down from London for the weekend because the climate was mild and the course, being surrounded by evergreens, looked more or less the same as in summer when the winter sun shone.

That was the set-up at many golf clubs in southern England, given that Ferndown also had the advantage of a holiday trade. In the North it was a little bit different, largely because the climate made it so; in the wilds of Yorkshire it could well happen that the pro was unable to earn anything at all for four to ten weeks in the year because of snow, and was completely dependent on his retainer during that period. If the retainer was £3–£4 a week, he could just about scrape by (he would only have an assistant in the busy part of the year). But – and here we return to Henry Longhurst's point – he had to have generous support from the members in the warmer months, and maintain a regular flow of income from lessons and matches as well as equipment.

For a long time, one of the main obstacles in a professional's life was that he could not advertise. This placed him at a great disadvantage with the sports shops which could advertise regularly in the newspapers and, if they were part of a chain, had much more buying muscle than any golf pro working on his own.

The best he could do was put on a sale at his shop, with posters in the window saying 'PRE-CHRISTMAS SALE – 20% OFF' or whatever. Then, if a visitor to the club stopped by and bought something, he was in luck; but otherwise he had no direct way of reaching the general public. He was not allowed to solicit the business of outsiders.

Now, thanks to the Office of Fair Trading, he is not restricted to selling goods only within the confines of the club. The commercial opportunities for an enterprising young professional are much better than they were; but it is a very competitive field because of the sports shops and discount houses, and the glossy offers in the magazines. To trade profitably, the professional needs a lot of cash, and access to further cash.

At least the club does not mind. The club is very happy to give its professional a shop rent-free and see him make a success of it. As long as everything goes well, the club benefits from the extra kudos of having the best golf shop in the neighbourhood, the members get a good deal on the things they buy, and the committee can be fairly sure that the professional won't come pestering them for a larger retainer.

All the same, it *is* a battle, and I do wonder how some of the young professionals manage to finance themselves, and whether this economic struggle isn't taking up too much of their time and disturbing the balance of what they should be doing at the club. Stocking a club shop is not so very different from

the price of a small flat. You won't get a lot for £20,000; £30,000 would be better, and then, if it's well displayed, with posters and so on, you can get by. But if you go to one of the big pro shops, you are looking at stuff worth a great deal more, maybe up to £70,000. Then there is the further snag, which affects all golf shops: are you turning it over quickly enough? You need a pretty hefty trade to sustain a large stock; remember, too, that there may be a few weeks in winter when trade ranges between very thin and nil.

A picture emerges of a man eternally trying to juggle too many balls at the same time. Perhaps that is a little pessimistic: all businesses carry risks, all have their ups and downs, their bumper weeks and their barren ones. But it does seem to me that we place too much emphasis on the commercial abilities of the professional, and in doing so we risk losing out on his abilities as a *teacher* and friend, and his important role in helping the members to play better golf and so increase their enjoyment of the game.

It is a perplexing subject, and the balance between getting it right and failure is finely drawn. Let me, however, suggest two resolutions for next season. They are drawn from Henry Longhurst's 'Unwritten Contract' and, thirty years on, I cannot fault them. The first concerns equipment, and asks every club member to:

'...resolve never again to buy a ball, a club, a pair of shoes or waterproofs, a trolley or any item of golfing equipment whatever, from anyone except his own club Pro.'

The second goes further:

'It ought to be a tradition in every club, as it is in some, that the professional is never without a game on Sunday mornings.'

Thank you, gentlemen...and ladies!

ell, why not? It's a big subject. Half our golf shots are played on the green, and putting undoubtedly generates more nervous strain and brain damage than any other activity on the course. Consequently, more books have been written about it than any other aspect of play, especially if you include all those volumes on 'inner golf' which are really instruction manuals on how to putt.

A

Alliss, Percy British professional golfer. In the 1933 Ryder Cup, on the sixteenth green at Southport and Ainsdale, unwitting victim of the Man on the MACKINTOSH (q.v.).

Alliss, Peter British professional golfer and television commentator. Son of Percy ALLISS. Better known for his long game.

Any fool can do it the second time Revered golf cliché meaning that you only live once on the putting surface. Miss those chances and you've had it.

Apron Entrance to the GREEN, usually cut more closely than the fairway but not as finely as the green itself.

Away You are 'away' if your ball is further from the hole than your opponent's.

B

Ball mark A small hole on the putting surface caused by a ball landing. You are allowed to repair damage caused by the impact of a ball, but you will not win friends if you start redesigning the landscape.

Ball marker A disc used to mark the position of a ball that is lifted on the putting surface. Remember the drill: it's 'Disc down, ball up', with the disc placed *behind* the ball. When you are ready to play, it's 'Ball down, disc away.' And not vice-versa.

Billiard cue Some bright spark at the US Amateur Championship of 1895, played at Newport, Rhode Island, thought he would be able to putt straighter using a billiard cue. The US Golf Association, formed the year before, was asked for a ruling, and they outlawed the billiard cue. The next putting rumpus was to be over the SCHENECTADY PUTTER.

C

Calamity Jane Famous putter used by Bobby Jones in many of his championship wins. Its origins are disputed, but there is no doubt it was a rusting museum piece when Jones first laid hands on it. Calamity Jane had a rather lofted blade, and a hickory shaft which had been broken in two places and bound with whipping. Immediately he began using it/her, Jones started holing his putts with remarkable consistency, and he and Calamity Jane became inseparable.

Campbell, Sir Guy Golf course architect and grand old character, responsible for these wise words: 'There is a master spot on the line of each putt. Find it, and see that the ball is so hit that it runs over it.' Many of today's champions use this technique, including Jack Nicklaus.

Chambers, Doris Fine golfer and twice captain of Britain's Curtis Cup team. She wrote: 'Lucky are those who can concentrate without effort.' Lucky indeed, especially on the green when the chips are down and the crowd won't stop buzzing. However, too much concentration can get you into trouble as well.

Constant, Archie Golfer of the old school who said: 'If you want to be a good putter, you have to get down to it and study the line from both ends.' So there you are. Just don't take half an hour doing it, that's all.

Crabb, Arthur Another golden oldie. Many moons ago he wrote: 'What good is the best of long games if you can't sink putts. Golf matches today are won and lost on the greens.' Sounds like a cry from the heart, doesn't it? I'm with you, Arthur!

D

Devotee, A Mystery commentator (female?) who had this to say: 'The beauty of golf, the *moral* beauty of golf lies greatly in this: that while self-consciousness is calamitous, self-assurance is fatal.' Just chew that one over next time you are

putting to save a match.

Drive for show, putt for dough Motto carved on the grey matter of most professional golfers.

E

Etiquette Ninety-nine per cent of etiquette is common sense. As far as behaviour on the putting green goes: when removing the flagstick, try not to hurl it across the green like a javelin. Keep your bag and trolley well out of the

way. Watch what your shadow is doing. Be kind to the putting surface – after all, it didn't acquire that beautiful manicured look overnight; the way some people charge around on the greens, I can almost hear the grass scream.

F

Freeze When forces unknown prevent you from moving the putter back and playing the shot. A common condition among the over-forties, when age, marital stress and acoholic beverages begin to exact their price. See also TWITCH, YIPS.

Fulford, Harry Golfer and golf philosopher, who wrote: 'Follow through with your putts. NEMESIS will overtake you for stopping the progress of the club as soon as you strike the ball.'

G

Gimme What your real friends say when they are left with a putt of up to four feet.

Gobbler A putt that flies into the hole and which, had it missed, would have gone a long way past. Literally, the hole 'gobbles' the ball.

Green The surface which has been prepared for putting. Not to be confused with the expression 'through the green', which in the RULES OF GOLF refers to the whole area of the course.

Greenstaff Employees at golf clubs who maintain the course. Since the post-war social revolution, such positions are regarded as quite cushy numbers. Greenstaff now come to work in cars instead of cycling up from the village! They enjoy all manner of perks and privileges such as overalls, dressing time, washing-up time, a cold water tap, four rolls of loo paper a year (supplied free!) and even a converted oil barrel for use as a brazier during the winter months only. Yes, greenstaff are pressing to join the New Elite!

H

Holderness, Sir Eric Distinguished amateur golfer. He wrote: 'When one sees a ball go off the face of the putter in a timid and irresolute manner, it is clear evidence that the putter is slowing down when it hits.' A good point; the putter must be accelerating at the moment of impact, or the shot will lack control.

Hole 'What it's all about, Peter' – or so they tell me! More precisely, it's a can-shaped receptacle officially measuring '4¼ inches in diameter and at least 4 inches deep.' See also MARSLAND, H., RIM.

Hole-in-one When the tee-shot goes straight into the hole. The odds against doing it are said to be about 2000-1.

I

Irish professional Usually a man of peculiar vision. Said an IP to a client: 'You must remember, Sorr, that when you are looking down on the ball you can see only two-thirds of it. The other two-thirds is out of sight, and that's the part you must aim at.' Except, of course, when putting, or during the mating season.

K

Kirkaldy, Hugh British Open Champion, 1891. His wooden putter became the trophy of the President's Putter, the annual match play competition of the Oxford and Cambridge Golfing Society; each year the ball used by the winner is attached to the putter by a silver chain.

L

Left-hand-below-right The wrong-way-round putting grip which several golfers, myself included, have resorted to in times of crisis. Bernhard Langer is probably the best-known golfer currently putting with his left hand down the shaft.
Line The ideal path along which your putt should travel to the hole.
Lowe, H. Wise man who wrote: 'The art of putting consists in hitting the ball with freedom, grace and accuracy right in the middle of the club.' What could be simpler? And yet, for a lot of golfers, it's *too* simple. They have to be fiercely technical – elbows out, special grip, pressure here, pressure there, plus clubs that look like a set of abortionist's tools. See also MAGIC PUTTER.

M

Mackintosh, man on the Unknown bounder responsible for my father going one down against Gene SARAZEN in the 1933 Ryder Cup. For full story, see chapter 'On Watching Golf'.
Magic putter What millions of golfers are searching for at any one time. If only they can find *it*, their game will be transformed. Or so they like to think. It never will, because whenever a putter is needed, some fallible human being has to come along, grip it and take a pass at the ball. That is where the secret lies – in TOUCH AND FEEL. Some folks have it, and some folks keep buying new putters.
Marsland, H. Golf thinker and inventor. He wrote to me with ingenious plans for a new way of cutting holes which, if it worked, would eliminate the problem of the rim being raised and stopping putts which otherwise would have squeaked in. As he explains, 'Holes are cut by a tool which cuts the total diameter of the hole in one go, through a board on which the greenkeeper stands.' This, he says, is not the best way to do it because 'if you push anything into a green, you create pressure. Although the cutting tool blade is admittedly thin, there must be some

pressure build-up in the land. When the tool is pulled out, the pressures built up relieve themselves and – just in odd cases – the lip of the hole is raised.' He also queries whether a twelve-stone man standing on a small board may not also create additional pressures, enough to exaggerate some small unevenness in the ground. I will not reveal the solutions he proposes, in case I want to go into business with him, but I certainly think he is on to something.

Matthews, W.J. Golf enthusiast, who at the age of 82 passed on this tip to me. 'If you want to be a good putter, hit the ball on the right line and the right weight, and it will go in the hole. All you have to do first is to make up your mind about the line and the weight, and that is a question of personal judgment. Elementary, my dear Watson.' That's all very well, Sir, if you have a superb eye and are a wonderful mathematician, and never FREEZE, TWITCH or get the YIPS. But at my age, let alone yours, it ain't always so elementary.

N

Nemesis Goddess of divine retribution. See also Harry FULFORD.

Never up, never in A phrase to cheer the faint-hearted, meaning that if you don't hit your putts firmly enough to reach the hole, they cannot possibly go in. For as long as you live the hole will *never* come towards the ball. Not many people know that!

O

Old pawky The favourite putter of the great Willie PARK. Long retired, it now hangs in the clubhouse at Woking GC, adorned with Willie's own testimony: 'It holed mony a guid putt.'

P

Park, Willie (Junior) Famous Scottish golfer who, as the author of *The Art of Putting* (1920), has a lot to answer for. The trouble with Willie was that he not only knew what he was talking about, he could do it as well. He was a straightforward man, and a great believer in self-confidence. 'Confidence is a great essential to putting,' he wrote, 'and confidence can always be got by practice.' Personally, I am not too sure about that, but maybe it works for some.

Of course, putting styles were very different in Willie's day, as were the putting surfaces (see SCYTHE). Today you would not find someone saying that 'The club should only hit the ball, not the ball and the ground. Even after the ball has been hit, the club should not touch the ground.' On the other hand, much of what he had to say about the principles of putting still hold good. For example: 'A two-foot downhill putt is much more difficult to hole than a four-foot uphill putt.' Now that is one of the eternal truths.

Pin Popular name for the flagstick.

Pin-high When the ball is just about level with the hole, and any distance to either side of it.

Q

Quit This means to hold back on a shot and not play firmly through the ball. Usually a prelude to disaster.

R

Rim Where the unlucky putter sees his ball come to rest, hanging over the very edge of the hole instead of dying graciously in it. See also MARSLAND, H.

Rules You are meant to know these, and I do not propose to trespass on the territory of the R & A by repeating them here. Broadly speaking, as they affect putting:

– You are not allowed to draw chalk lines between your ball and the hole.

– Portable Hoovers are not permitted for removing 'loose impediments'; you must pick them up or brush them aside with your hand.

- Replace all divots before playing your next shot.
- When your ball overhangs the hole, you are not allowed to blow it in.
- If your ball goes in off another player's ball during a stroke play competition, this is not a cause for celebration and punching the air with your fist; it will also cost you two strokes.

S

Sarazen, Gene Fine American golfer who wrote: 'The lie of the putter should be one so that you can stand directly over the ball looking down on to it. Unless you do this your putting stroke will necessarily be erratic.' Well, many ideas have changed since those words were written. Nowadays people don't seem to mind how they stand – so long as the thing goes in.

Schenectady putter A revolutionary centre-shafted putter, invented by an employee of the General Electric Company who worked at their plant in Schenectady, New York. In 1904 Walter Travis created a stir when he used one of these 'croquet mallets' to win the British Amateur Championship. In 1909 the R & A decided the Schenectady was not a golf club and it was banned in Britain until 1952. In the United States it has always been legal.

Scythe When we read about how they putted in the old days, it is important to remember that most greens were rugged places. Before the cylinder mower came into use, greens were cut by men using scythes. They shaved the surface down as best they could, but obviously they did not have the techniques of grasscutting and watering, the weedkillers, fertilizers and so on which enable today's greenstaff to bring on a putting surface and have it in perfect condition just when they want it. At best, putting surfaces in the Willie Park era were like a reasonably-kept lawn. At worst, well, it's no wonder that putters in those days were slightly lofted; up in the air was the safest place to be.

Sex Have you noticed how some people can't keep sex out of putting? They belong to the 'My Putter Is A Woman' school; to become a member, all they have to do is admit that they haven't a clue about how to succeed on the green. This leaves them free to develop all kinds of daft theories about their failures. For example:

'Putters are very feminine and capricious. They are fickle and sensitive. No club is so human as a putter. None so worthy of the name of "friend" if true, but none more likely to do you an injury if disloyal and treacherous. Like so many of her sex the putter has a touch of vanity in her which must be humoured if she is to be won as a faithful mistress.'

In other words, they transfer all the blame for their rotten performances on to a poor defenceless piece of metal. But why pick on the putter? Why can't it just do the job it was built for, like all the other clubs in the bag? I think the main reason people get obsessive about their putters is that they think they are seeing too much of them – a bit like the wife, I agree, but I have noticed something else about this blame-shifting business. Only men do it. Female golfers don't try to take it out on their putters, or on any other club for that matter. You never find, even at the nineteenth hole, a lady member crying:

'My driver, he's a *real* man! He's so long and strong, sometimes I go giddy at the top of my backswing...'

Of course not. They are much more sensible than generations of male golf writers have led us to believe.

Simplex A centre-shafted putter modelled on the SCHENECTADY. When Andrew Kirkaldy, the professional at St Andrews, was shown a Simplex putter, his verdict was: 'I wud sooner play wi' a tay spoon!'

T

Touch and feel The enviable ability to pop in your putts using a very basic technique. This ability exists in the most unexpected people – an old pensioner, say, going round in his wellies can leave far better-equipped golfers standing when it comes to the simple yet very complex business of putting straight and true – and doing it time after time.

Twitch Putting affliction, related to FREEZE and almost identical to the YIPS. There are basically two kinds of twitch. One is a general feeling of nervousness and incipient panic: in some the facial muscles may be affected, giving rise to a

tic whose rhythm increases on the approach to a green. The second kind of twitch is the putting action itself; the moment of freeze has been overcome and the putter is drawn back. Now the shot is played: with a jerking, twitchy motion, the putter is sent skewing at the ball which, in turn, goes anywhere but straight.

W

Wilson, William Golf enthusiast who wisely wrote: 'Every golfer should aim at irreproachable green manners. Speaking plainly, he should do nothing to annoy his opponent. Self-confidence and concentration are the first essentials of a fine game. Neither can be possessed if your mind is divided between wishing your opponent ill and your own play.'

Wry-necked putter This was a kind of substitute for the centre-shafted putter when these were illegal (see SCHENECTADY PUTTER). It had a kink in the neck of the shaft which brought it more in line with the centre of the head.

Y

Yips, the This is the dreaded condition described under TWITCH. There is no certain cure. Two years on a health farm might help (no golf, naturally). In the first book in this series (*Bedside Golf*) I described how Henry Longhurst and I distinguished between the 'Semprini', the form of yip where the ball ripples away to the right, and the 'Winifred Attwell', where the right hand overtakes the left at a tremendous rate and the ball squirts off to the left. It can be quite fun spotting the Semprinis and the Winnie Attwells out on the course – though not so hilarious when it happens to you.

Yet More Clubhouse Tales

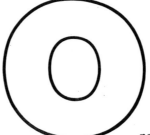

ne of the best stories about the late Ben Sayers, Senior, the great player and clubmaker from North Berwick, relates how he sold two left-handed and two right-handed clubs to a rather snooty American visitor who seemed to think the game of golf was rather beneath him.

Several hours later, the American marched up to Sayers and complained bitterly that he had been made a fool of.

'Oh, no, Sir,' said Sayers. 'It's quite in order. What you do is, you take the right-handed clubs for the holes going out and you change over and use the left-handed clubs coming in.'

Not Stopping

At Arcot Hall, there used to be a lake at the side of the ninth green, not far from the clubhouse. One day, after a dreadful round, one of the more ardent members was seen to go over to the lake, raise his bag of clubs above his head and throw it into the lake.

After a few quick whiskies at the bar, taken alone, he got up, walked back to the lake, took off his shoes and socks, rolled up his trousers and waded into the water. When he came out with his bag of clubs, several onlookers thought he had regretted his hasty decision. They were wrong. He unzipped a pocket in the side of the bag, took out his car keys, flung the bag of clubs back into the lake and was never seen at the golf club again.

The Reluctant Flasher

At the Walker Cup Dinner at Turnberry in 1963, an American was asked how one of his compatriots was playing these days.

'Oh,' came the reply, 'he's just about given up the game. Of course, he was never basically sound, you know. His grip was all wrong. It reminded me of

a man trying to relieve himself behind a tree without anybody seeing.'

A Bag Of Miracles

During the Italian Campaign a group of soldiers had been on the march for several days. They came across a small town called Cassino. As it was Sunday, they all went to church. The service began and they took out their prayer books – all except one man (a Coloured Jewish Eskimo) who took out a golf bag and began chipping balls into the font.

'Soldier!' ordered the Sergeant (who was also Jewish – you could tell by his blue suede boots), 'put away those clubs already.'

After the service, the soldier was brought before his CO who said:

'I hope you have an explanation for playing golf in church, and also a letter from your secretary, otherwise I shall punish you as no man has been punished before.'

'Sir,' said the soldier, 'we have been on the march for six days now, and I have no Bible or prayer book – only my golf bag.

'You see, when I take out my driver, I think of the Israelites being driven out into the Wilderness.

'When I take out my three-iron (with heel-toe balance and a bigger sweetspot) I remember that God has a big sweetspot for everyone.

'When I take out my five-iron, I think of the Ten Commandments – half of them.

'When I take out my six-iron, I remember the parable of the wise virgins: six made the party and six weren't really virgins at all – just a bunch of Variety girls up from Jerusalem on a hot-dogger.

'When I look at my waterproofs, I am reminded that God will protect me from everything.

'When I look at my scorecard, I think of Confession, and when I stand downwind from my caddie I am reminded of the stable where Jesus was born.

'So you see, Sir, my golf bag has served me as a Bible and a prayer book as well as a golf bag. You want to feel it?'

The soldier was court-marshalled for gross insolence and given a choice of sentence. Either he could face a firing squad, or be sentenced to ten years of listening to Harry Carpenter playing excerpts from Handel's *Messiah* on a set of engine tappets and a valve spring compressor.

I know. I was the vicar.

(This was written by a former assistant of mine, Derrick Kuhler, when he was with me at Moor Allerton. Some names have been omitted to protect the guilty!)

Frogmarching in Scotland

A Frenchman arrived at St Andrews and went to the starter's box to book a time for the following day. The starter asked for his name.

'Fouquet,' said the Frenchman.

'What did you say?' asked the starter.

'Fouquet,' repeated the Frenchman.

'Aye, well ye'll be here at eight-thirty in the morn,' said the starter, 'and when I call "Ferrguson", ye'll play away.'

Crisis Management

I am indebted to Leslie Jones of Filey, past president of the English Golf Union, for a pair of true stories about slowcoaches on the golf course and how to deal with them. The first incident took place on 30th August, 1939, five days before Britain went to war with Germany, and Leslie was playing in a fourball which

included the editor of the *Newcastle Journal*.

Although it was a generally quiet afternoon, they caught and were then continually held up by a slow fourball in front. When they were on the sixth tee, a caddie came from the clubhouse on a bicycle with a note for the editor. He read it, then quickly wrote another which he gave to the caddie, asking him to take it to the people in front. On receiving the note, they showed more urgency than they had done all afternoon, and waved Leslie and his party through.

They completed their round and were still in the clubhouse, minus the editor who had made his farewells, when the other fourball rolled slowly in. Leslie asked one of them what had been in the note which the caddie had given them. He produced it and handed it over. It read:

'I have just had word from my office that Hitler is digging trenches in the Mediterranean and they would like me in the office as soon as possible to report the crisis.'

On the second occasion, fourballs were again the root of the problem. It was a busy weekend and the match behind Jones & Co had already driven into them twice when they came to a big hold-up at the thirteenth tee. Coming face to face with the encroachers (a notorious group of bandits), they gave warning that if they drove into them again they would knock their ball away.

Minutes later, while Leslie and his friends were waiting for the green to clear so they could play their second shots, a ball trickled amongst them, followed by a second. Leslie took out a seven-iron and knocked one of the balls over the hedge, deep into no-man's land. He waited for the offending players to come up and said to them:

'We warned you. If you want your ball, it's over there.'

One of them took it rather badly: 'Right. Two can play at that game,' he snarled, took out a club and knocked the ball nearest to him over the hedge.

'Have it your own way,' said Leslie. 'That was your brother George's ball.'

Leslie's experiences remind me of the story about the two very wayward golfers. They were all over the place, and tempers were distinctly frayed when someone drove into them. This sent them into an even worse rage. As they waited for the offending player, their eyes were popping out of their heads.

'Sorry,' said the chap breezily, as he came up to them, 'I didn't know you belonged to this hole.'

Learning the Hard Way

At a certain well-known club, a busy main road runs parallel with the third hole. A player hooked his tee shot which shattered the windscreen of a double-decker

bus which swerved and crashed into an approaching lorry. Meanwhile several cars in each direction concertinaed into each other and two cyclists and some pedestrians became involved. The place was like a battlefied within minutes.

The accident services were quickly on the scene and the golfers had gone through a gate leading on to the road to try to help some of the injured. A senior policeman had taken charge and he came across to the golfers, saying:

'I understand that one of you was responsible for this lot.'

'Yes, it was my tee shot,' admitted one of them.

'Well, what are you going to do about it?' asked the policeman.

'It must be my grip that's wrong,' answered the culprit. 'I'll have to try to get my right hand a bit further round the shaft.'

Platform Golf

Back in the Twenties, when there were hardly any cars on the roads, it is a wonder that some out-of-the-way courses were used at all, except by a handful of locals and their sheep. Fortunately, this was long before the good Dr Beeching made so free with his axe, and the railway map of Britain was still a thriving tree with trunk lines, branch lines and sub-branches running just about everywhere. Given the will, carless people could still get to within a mile or two of some of the remoter courses.

The only trouble with trains is that they won't come when you whistle for them. In order to reach one of those desirable links courses to the east of Edinburgh, people used to have to wait up to half an hour at a small junction a couple of miles from the course.

One cold, wet March afternoon there were only two men on the platform, which had no shelter, and that day the train was at least twenty minutes late. In the end, one poor chap could bear the silence no longer. Although they had not been introduced, he stumped up to the other fellow and, gesturing across the fields, said:

'Dash it, I've been a member over there for thirty years, and during that time I reckon I've spent eight months at this blasted station!'

The Army Game

The priest and an old major were playing a round of golf. It was not the priest's day, and some of his shots slowed them down to such a degree that the major could not stop himself from uttering a few fruity comments, laced with traditional oaths, which rather upset the priest.

'I think, Sir,' he remonstrated stiffly, 'that if you have no respect for yourself, you might at least show respect for the cloth.'

'Hang it all, man!' thundered the major. 'We're playing golf, not billiards!'

Every Dog His Day

The new captain of the Motor Traders Golf Society was about to drive in at

Sunningdale. According to his version of events, about fifty-two caddies were ranged at various vantage points on or near the first fairway, poised to retrieve the ball and so win the traditional reward – at one time a golden sovereign but by then 'a beggarly one pound note'.

A fifty-third caddie had been bribed by a previous captain to climb a tree not far from the tee and swing up and down like an ape to try and put the new man off his stroke. In vain. He hit an unusually good shot down the middle of the fairway, and a swarm of caddies converged on the ball.

Just then, from an adjacent garden, a black retriever dashed out and disappeared among the forest of legs, reappearing a few moments later with the captain's ball in its mouth. Pursued by several frustrated caddies, it galloped back along the eighteenth fairway. There, raking the bunker which protects the hole, was a very ancient greenkeeper. The dog ran up to him, dropped the ball at his feet and stood there wagging its tail. The old boy twigged what had happened when he saw the horde of caddies hallooing and puffing in his direction. He promptly picked up the ball and toddled off to the captain for his reward, which he duly got.

So, the race is not always to the swift – and we trust the dog collected a small commission.

Blind Faith

George's partner was mystified. 'Look,' he said, 'first you slice your ball into the bushes, then you hook it across the road, and now you've knocked it into the woods. Each time you hit the ball into the next county, you insist on chasing after it. Why?'

George gave his partner a pained look: 'It's my lucky ball.'

Shop Golf

Strange though it may seem, one of the first great promoters of golf was a firm of Glasgow outfitters. On Monday, 3rd March, 1924 the House of Rowan in Buchanan Street opened a sports department that was no ordinary sports department. To run it, they signed up a small squad of men who had made their names in golf, football, hockey, tennis and cricket, and then they announced to an astonished world that the 'Big Four' – James Braid, George Duncan, J.H. Taylor and Harry Vardon, no less – would be there on opening day and throughout the first week to give advice to all-comers. On the following Saturday they played in a sponsored fourball at Killermont, headquarters of the Glasgow Golf Club.

It was a Golden Age, and not just for golf. Later in the month Rowans gave their sales of cricket gear a timely pre-season boost by producing Jack Hobbs, J.W. Hearne and Herbert Sutcliffe. The great men arrived, and hundreds poured in for a free cricket lesson.

I am reminded of all this because I have been going through Rowans' own press cuttings books from the 1920s and '30s – a fascinating exercise because it shows that they were really very bold for their day. They did not get the services of all those wily champions for nothing, and yet they believed strongly enough in the future of big-time professional sport, and especially golf, to start all sorts of attractions and enterprises. In 1925 they staged a fourball at Gleneagles with George Duncan and Abe Mitchell playing the Americans Macdonald Smith and Joe Kirkwood, and in 1926 they broke all records with a Golf Week that featured Ted Ray, George Duncan, J.H. Taylor, Sandy Herd, James Braid and Harry Vardon. In 1927 they opened a branch in Birmingham, and by now at all the major tournaments they had a classy-looking stand in the exhibition marquee to show off their sweaters, scarves, shoes, and what you will.

The best was yet to come. In October 1930 Rowans introduced 'Fairway', a nine-hole indoor golf course laid out in the basement of the shop and 'playable by electric light'. It had five putting holes and four which were a chip and a putt with miniature trees to chip over, a lake, and bunkers made with

real sand. If you landed in a bunker, by the way, and were trapped, it cost you a penalty stroke to lift and drop.

Later that same month, Rowans opened a second Fairway course at their Birmingham store, and Messrs Vardon and Taylor – with 11 Open Championships between them – played a medal round.

The Fairway game was the first of its kind in Britain, but not in the world. The material used for the playing surface – cotton seed husks, dyed green – gives a clue to the origins of the game – the United States, where a small craze was taking hold for 'portable' versions of golf.

In 1933 Rowans acquired another import from the United States – their new resident professional, a Scot returned from exile by the name of James A. Smith. What Mr Smith had to say about the American approach to the game is very revealing:

'Over here,' Smith told the Glasgow *Daily Record*, 'we take our games mostly in the spirit of relaxation, and, whilst we do our best to succeed, we do not, as a rule, make a toil of a pleasure.

'Americans cannot look on games from this point of view. They wish to succeed and, to do so, are prepared to spend long hours of drudgery and hard work over every type of shot until mastery is gained.'

Not much has changed there. We British have become a little harder, perhaps, but the gulf is still wide, particularly at club and top amateur level. Which is the better way? That is for every individual to decide, but for my money there is another gulf which ought to be preserved, and that is the one between the tournament professional and the club player.

The professionals must be concerned with winning, otherwise they would not be able to stay on the circuit. It is the average club player I am a little

bit worried about. These days there is rather too much emphasis on winning and less about having fun; too much middling to heavy wagering and not enough of those silly little bets made on the spur of the moment for about 10p. I can understand a shift in attitudes to the point where, as they do, more people now write in to the R & A for rulings because they are keen to get things right and they also like to win their matches. But not to the point where it is regarded as slightly odd to show courtesy towards an opponent, as if that was a sign of weakness.

No, I can't be doing with that. Perhaps we should spend a little more time thinking about what we are up to – turn back the clubhouse clock to more spacious days and remember, as James A. Smith put it more than half a century ago, to 'take our games mostly in the spirit of relaxation'.

On Watching Golf

I t is always a great joy to hear people describe some special moment which they witnessed in a far-off tournament – and have never forgotten. The nostalgic view does tend to be a shade rosy, but those first encounters with golf and the great heroes of the game – as with first kisses and other delights – always seem to stay longer and more vividly in the memory.

Gordon McFall, who wrote to me from Dunmow, looked back with special pleasure to 'the days when you could walk round beside your heroes in the Open, keeping just a yard or two from them hearing their every remark and touching the magic clubs – till the caddie told you to bugger off'.

In those days he lived near the golf course at Formby, and well remembers the first time he saw wooden peg tees. 'They were used by Hagen and Al Watrous and I thought "The Haig" must be very, very rich as he never bothered to pick them up; so, darting forward on each tee after he'd played, I collected the lot.'

Hagen seems to figure more prominently in people's memories than any other player of his generation. His colourful ways, his language, and supreme confidence – plus his habit of winning – almost guaranteed him the attention of the crowds who thronged the tees. These were not roped off, remember, and people used to encroach almost up to the tee itself. Walter Hagen always saw to it that his swing would not be impeded, and that he would not have to decapitate anyone when he played his shot. He did this by stepping a yard or so behind the marker discs and starting a slow backswing, which had the effect of moving the spectators far enough from him and the other players. One day a spectator asked him:

'Am I all right standing here?'

'Sure,' relied Hagen. 'You're fine.' He pointed down the fairway. 'I'm going thataway.'

Hagen could never have been called an early-to-bed man. One night before a £500-a-side match against George Duncan, he was drinking whisky, smoking cigars and playing poker in his hotel at two o'clock in the morning. Someone said to him:

'It's time you packed up and went to bed, Walter. Your opponent's been in bed for hours.'

'Yeah,' replied Hagen, 'I betcha he's not sleeping.'

Another old-time spectator recalls standing at Carnoustie on the little hill beside the sixteenth green during the 1937 Open. In those days the Championship finished on a Friday and now it was early evening on the Thursday. Henry Cotton was going down the seventeenth with John McReady, the Edinburgh amateur. Also watching were 'The Great Walter', then non-playing captain of the US Ryder Cup team, and a number of his team, including Sam Snead and Byron Nelson.

'There he goes,' said Hagen. 'That is the man you will all be chasing for second place tomorrow.'

'How right he was,' my informant goes on. 'Henry won the next day in a lashing downpour of rain. He won with a score of 290 which was a tremendous effort. I can well remember I was soaked to the skin twice that day, just like Toots and a lot of the crowd.'

Hagen won his first Open Championship in 1922 – the splendid successor to Taylor, Vardon and Braid who since the turn of the century had largely made the trophy their own. Now almost a legend is the story of how, at Hoylake, Hagen holed his putt for a four at the eighteenth: '...He didn't look up to see if the ball went into the hole but merely cupped his ear with his hand to hear it rattle in. As he left the green, a spectator said to him:

'"Didn't you know, Walter, that was for the Championship?"
'"I had no fears," said Hagen. "No-one ever beat me in a play-off."'

The Man on the Mackintosh

In the last two or three years we have had one or two nasty cases of crowd
participation, when some member of the public has decided to stop his hero's
ball from running into further trouble, or niftily side-flicked the opposition
under a gorse bush. Personally, I have mixed views on whether or not we should
bring back hanging – but if we did, people like that would be top of my list for
the ultimate drop.

If it is any consolation to Graham Marsh and other recent victims of
spectator skulduggery, I can only say that it has been going on for years – even
as far back as my father's day! Of course, it is extremely difficult to establish
whether the interception was done with malice in mind or whether it was purely
accidental, arising from stupidity or some sudden paralysis of the limbs, as when
the rabbit freezes before the snake. In the old days, too, as we have seen, people
were roped off a lot less at the big tournaments, so were more likely to present
random targets for stray balls.

Gordon McFall wondered whether my father Percy had ever told me of one such incident in which he was involved, adding: 'Maybe he never knew!' Well, if he had never found out, ignorance would surely have been bliss. Let my correspondent explain:

'It was in the Ryder Cup played at Southport and Ainsdale in 1933 – the first time Byron Nelson played there, and Walter Hagen was the non-playing captain.

'In the singles your father was playing Gene Sarazen and they came to the short sixteenth all-square. Your father had the honour and put his tee-shot about ten feet from the pin. I was standing behind the green and beside me was a man sitting on his mackintosh. Sarazen's shot was much too strong. It bounced on the green and was obviously destined for deep pussy-willow had not the oaf beside me leapt to his feet and picked up his mackintosh to try and get out of the way. The ball was caught up in his mac, and, not content with that, its owner gave it a violent flick which sent Sarazen's ball back on the green, laying your father a stymie to boot. Inevitably, Sarazen holed his putt and your father missed an eminently holeable one.

'Result: poor dear magnificent Percy one down with two to play instead of one up. He lost the match.'

Yes, I had heard about that one. But it was not in Father's nature to complain, bless him, or to envy others their success.

With Friends Like These…

For all his good nature, had my father been around today he might have had a thing or two to say about the way spectators behave on the course – especially in the States, but you get it here as well. I am thinking, in particular, of the noise they make. The Americans, with all their hoopin' and whoopin', take the biscuit, but we are aping them, and in my view all are degrading the game of golf.

At the Open, there has always been good applause on the eighteenth hole as the Championship came to an end. As the favourites walked towards the green – the Jacklins, Nicklauses, the Palmers and many others who weren't going to win – the cheering grew warmer, and then there was a special, longer round of applause as the new Champion arrived. Nowadays, it's more like Brighton beach on a Bank Holiday. Some people arrive hours in advance, racing each other for pole position, which they keep for the next twelve hours. They arrive laden with beer, flasks and sandwiches: they squat down, and for the rest of the day do nothing but make noise. Thank God they are in a minority.

It doesn't matter who is playing. If it's young Fred Bones from Burnley, who only just made the cut and is about to finish last – no matter, let's put our hands together (dreadful phrase, makes me think something is leaking) and cheer him in. 'Good boy, Fred! Well played, my son!' (*Bends down.*) 'Where did I put the opener, Vera? In me pocket? Oh.' (*Stands up and takes another swig.*) 'Yeah! That's my boy, Fred! Next year you'll kill 'em! Land of Ho-ope and Glor-ee…'

Poor bewildered Fred gets nearly as much applause as the Champion. No wonder he thinks he's a star. In that kind of atmosphere, everyone's a star.

Postscript Only days after I wrote these lines, my morning newspaper arrived with further tidings of spectator lunacy. Bernhard Langer was competing in the Bing Crosby tournament, and lying in about sixth position on the third day. He drove off at the tenth at Cypress Point, saw his ball come to rest on the fairway, then watched in amazement as a lady spectator picked it up, slipped it in her pocket and walked off. The marshalls caught her fairly quickly, but had the devil of a job persuading her to part with her souvenir. In the end she did and Langer played on.

So Who Wants to be Perfect?

O f course, you can be too serious about the whole thing. It is only a game, after all. It is not absolutely necessary to play every day, or even once a week. You don't have to belong to the ritziest club in the county and spurn all others, and you don't have to go there kitted out like the model in the mail-order catalogue, a fragrant vision in cashmere and alligator skin shoes, rounded off with chinchilla hood-covers.

There is a more relaxed way to play golf – and it need not involve flying down to Malaga or across to the Caribbean. The name of the game is knockabout golf, and you can virtually do it yourself.

The first thing to do is to purge your mind of the idea that golf is the *dolce vita* of sport, and that a good golf club has to be a palace of delights. In Britain you won't find a single golf palace, so you might as well stop looking. On the Continent, yes. But on the Continent they have a different attitude and are prepared to pay for their luxuries. In the United States they also don't mind the expense if they think it's good value and they are enjoying themselves. In Britain that is not the prevailing attitude.

Most people in this country think that golf should *not* be expensive. I agree. Then they spoil a good argument by complaining about the missing facilities at their club, where the subscription is the equivalent of £5 a week. (I will exempt the Jewish golf clubs from this because, under duress, the members can be persuaded to pay more. They want more, and when they can see that the cost is unlikely to be met out of someone else's pocket, they stump up.)

The result is that too many British golf clubs end up looking homogenized, uninteresting, with too little money to meet the aspirations of members who are already grumpy about having to pay £5 a week. If only more people would recognize that you can't have Chantilly for £5 a week. What you can have, though, is a marvellous knockabout club with a modest clubhouse, where the game of golf is the thing and the social side can be left to look after itself.

Campaign for Real Golf?

Plenty of clubs used to be shamelessly unpolished, and they were delightful places. Who cares if there is no Filipino barman to mix your favourite cocktail at the nineteenth hole. What's wrong with bringing a few beers with you instead. Who cares about showers and saunas and jacuzzis. You can have all that later, when you get home. The main thing is the golf and, with luck, the natural surroundings – the pine and heather, the flowing hills, the woodlands beyond, or a glimpse of the sea down some narrow combe...

Does any of this remind you of the good old days? It really should not be too difficult to recreate them, especially if there is a friendly landowner in your group. Just think of the Apple Tree Gang, those splendid pioneers who started the St Andrews Golf Club of Yonkers, New York, with a three-hole course laid out in the first president's cow pasture. That was how the first American golf club began, in 1888.

Perhaps you would prefer something a little more ready-made. Fine, but here it is important to avoid too many improvements too soon. Whatever form your club takes, the chief thing to watch out for is that it doesn't become too popular. Almost invariably, this kind of venture attracts a remarkable number of new friends and supporters. Then someone comes along and says:

'You know, we could really make this quite good.'

He goes on to explain that he has spoken to some of the lads and they would be prepared to come along at the weekends and help put in one or two bunkers. Then there's that old shed we use. Well, wouldn't it be nice to put up something a bit better; after all, we've got Joe the builder, and he could get the materials cheap.

In next to no time, you're on the way again, only this time you're breaking your back as well as paying out a lot more than you ever used to – all in order to make your little club like all the others. The crowning glory comes about twenty years later, when someone says:

'Be a good idea to put a billiard room on, you know.'

Now you've really made it!

An ideal example of the club I mean was described to me not long ago in a viewer's letter. Thank you, Ann Hamilton. I will not name the club, except to say that it is in Devon – not for fear that everyone will rush there and spoil it, but because I do not want to single out any one club and say: 'Look, this is the one. Make yours like this.' There must be hundreds of permutations on the theme, just as there are hundreds of pleasant little neighbourhood pubs that the brewers would do well to leave alone. See what you think of it:

' · ...It is a remarkable nine-hole course, the predominant occupants being sheep who undoubtedly do most of the mowing, except on the greens which are wired round, not against the sheep but against a herd of Highland cattle which are beautiful and very docile. There are no bunkers, but several shallow gulleys. At the far end of the course, just beyond the fourth green, you come to a beautiful bouldered stream, and at that point three pony riders passed us. The flag on the sixth green was virtually obliterated by the herd of cattle which had chosen that spot, ringing the green, for their morning cudding.

'I will never forget that morning's golf. It would have been worth the £3 green fee just to walk round the course, without playing. We gained an impression of a very happy course from the elderly gentleman to whom we paid our green fees, and from the six golfers we met while going round.'

Now that is what I call progress.

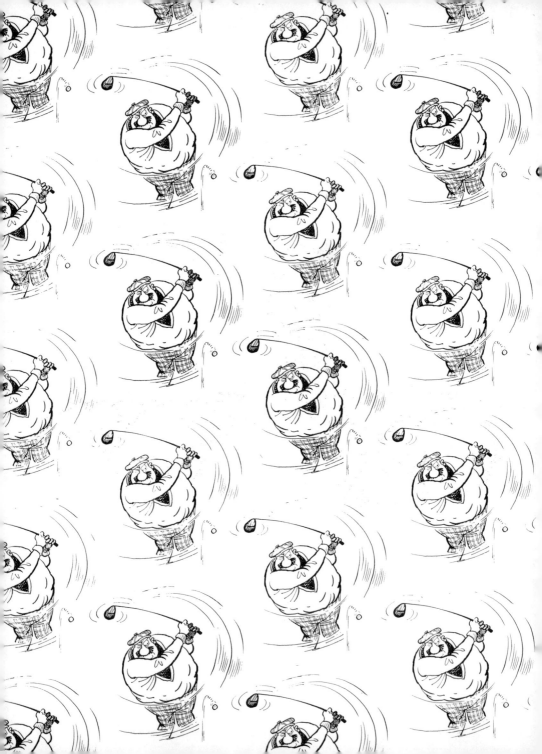

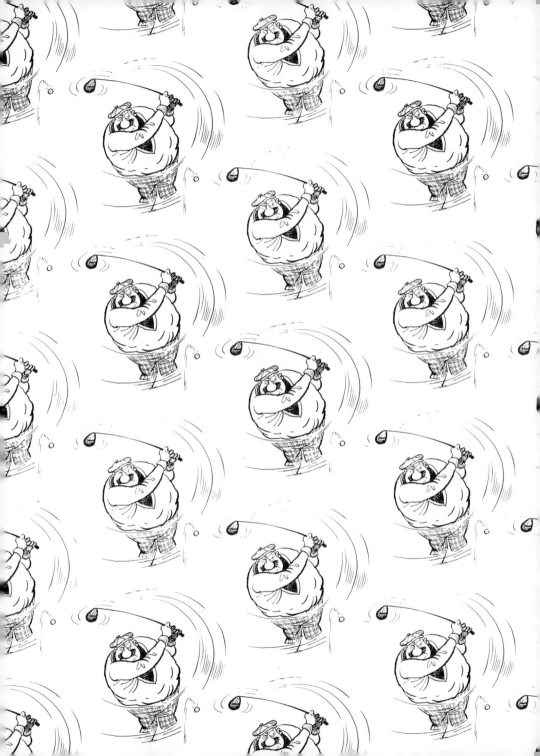